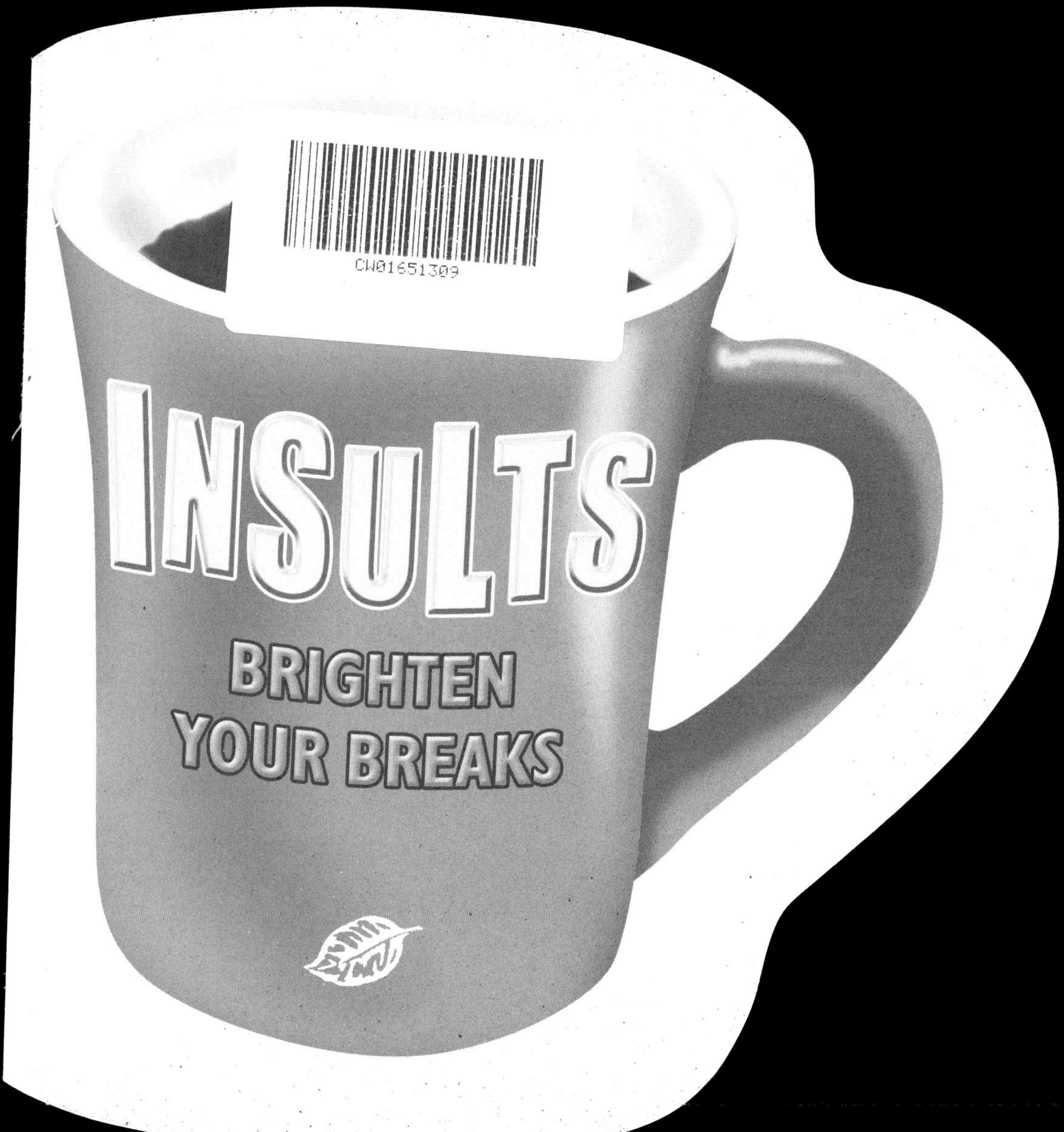
INSULTS
BRIGHTEN
YOUR BREAKS

Published in the UK in 2006
by Autumn Publishing Ltd,
Chichester, West Sussex, UK, PO20 7EQ.

Designed by Aimee Forde
Formatted by Ivan Finnegan
Compiled by Sonya Nikade

First published 2006
Printed in China 5 4 3 2 1

CONTENTS

INTRODUCTION

Whether you want to fling a casual insult at a colleague, or are just trying to get a rise from your mates, this little book will give you the perfect ammunition. You'll find insults for every type of person in your life – for the fat, the useless, the psychotic, the ugly, and for the just plain stupid…actually, especially for the just plain stupid. Be warned though – throw too many of these insults around and you might find yourself losing a friend or two…but if they're complete imbeciles, it's probably not that big a loss anyway.

Happy insulting!

Sonya Nikadie

Chapter 1

TO THE TOTALLY STUPID

Some of us are missing a whole banana from our lunchbox; some of us are a few slices short of a loaf. However you prepare your next meal, if you're a lettuce leaf short of a salad, some of these insults might be aimed directly at you.

You're so stupid...

You're depriving a village somewhere of its idiot.

If you donated your brain to science, they'd give it back.

When you collect your thoughts, they fit in a very small container.

During evolution your ancestors were in the control group.

You're knitting with only one needle.

Your carpet doesn't reach from wall to wall.

You're so stupid...

You're not digging in the same ditch as the rest of us.

You're so stupid...

Your fingers and toes are numbered.

When you heard 90% of all crimes occur around the home, you went out.

You need a cue card to say "Huh?"

You need instructions on how to use a rocking chair.

You planted a dogwood tree and expected a litter of puppies.

You play solitaire...for cash.

You're so stupid...

You'd trip over a cordless phone.

If I gave you a penny for your intelligence, I'd get change back.

You got hit by a parked car.

Even stupid people think you are slow.

If you had a brain you'd take it out and play with it.

When you dropped acid the car battery fell on your foot.

You're so stupid...

You're missing a layer of insulation in your attic.

When God said "Come forth for brains", you came fifth.

You donated your body to science...before you were done using it.

You're proof that evolution can go in reverse.

If brains were dynamite, you wouldn't have enough to blow the wax out of your ears.

You're so stupid...

You stared at the orange juice carton because it said 'concentrate'.

On forms that say 'sign here' you put 'Pisces'.

When you saw 'under 18 not admitted' at the cinema, you went out and brought back 17 friends.

Your clock is ticking, but it's not telling the time.

Your spark can't jump the gap.

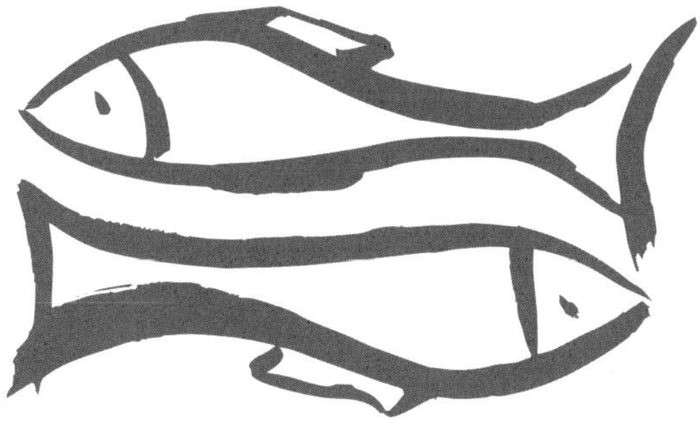

You're so stupid...

You make a black hole look bright.

Your receiver is off the hook.

Your lift is stuck between floors.

You move your lips to pretend you're reading.

You're not dealing from a full deck.

You're so stupid...

Your lights are on but nobody's home.

You're so stupid...

Not all your dogs are barking.

Your mooring lines don't reach the dock.

You're not the sharpest tool in the shed.

You're permanently out to lunch.

You're sitting in the right pew, but the wrong church.

You're so stupid...

You're not the shiniest penny in the jar.

You don't have enough sense to come in out of the rain.

You're not firing on all six cylinders.

You're not the brightest light in the harbour.

Your puzzle is missing a few pieces.

You're so stupid...

There's lots of silverware on your table, but no plates.

You're operating in stand-by mode.

You've got only one chopstick in the chow mein.

You ought to have a warning label on your forehead.

You were first in line for brains, but ended up holding the door open.

You're so stupid...

You're out of your depth in a puddle.

You're so stupid...

You have all your bricks, but no cement holding them together.

Your lift goes all the way to the top…but the door doesn't open.

Your dock doesn't quite reach the water.

There's plenty of salt in the shaker, but no holes in the cap.

The gates are down, the lights are flashing, but the train isn't coming.

You're so stupid...

You're suffering from clue deficit disorder.

You're strolling through life with one shoelace untied.

You don't have both oars in the water – you can't even find the damn boat.

You're missing a few buttons on your remote control.

Your radio doesn't pick up all the stations.

If you were any more stupid...

You'd have to be watered twice a week.

Short 'n' snappy

Sometimes, you just want to hand out your put-downs in as few breaths as possible. On the next two pages you'll find some quick 'n' sharp insults for just this very purpose.

You're...

A few beers short of a six-pack.

A few bricks short of a wall.

A few sandwiches short of a picnic.

A car short of a chase scene.

A chapter short of a novel.

As sharp as a doughnut dunked in coffee.

Short 'n' Snappy
You're...

A flower short of an arrangement.

A Brady short of a Bunch.

A sandwich short of a picnic.

A crouton short of a salad.

A snowflake short of a ski slope.

Chapter 2

TO THE HIDEOUSLY UGLY

If your enemies are as ugly as the north-facing end of a south-bound camel, you may want to use the gems on the following pages.

You're so ugly...

When you walk into a bank, they turn off the surveillance cameras.

When you went to enter an ugly contest, they said, "Sorry, no professionals."

When you looked out the window you got arrested for mooning.

Just after you were born, your mother said, "What a treasure!" and your father said, "Yes, let's go bury it."

You've got teeth like a row of condemned houses.

You're so ugly...

When you were born, the doctor slapped your mother.

You're so ugly...

People at the circus pay money not to see you.

You have a face only a mother could love – but she hates it too.

The last time I saw something that looked like you, I pinned a tail on it.

You threw a boomerang and it wouldn't even come back.

You get 364 extra days to dress up for Halloween.

You're so ugly...

When you walk into the kitchen, the rats jump on the table and start screaming.

You're so ugly...

The last time you heard a whistle was when you got hit by a train.

You didn't just get hit with the ugly stick, the whole ugly tree attacked you.

There are better heads on a butt full of pimples.

When you put on your lipstick, it keeps backing down the tube.

Chapter 3

TO THE TUBBIES AND CHUBBIES

Know someone who's a little on the hefty side? Someone who's a bit of a porker? If you have a pal who's carrying so many spare tyres he can't even jump to a conclusion, you'll find some conversation starters right here.

You're so fat...

When you turn around, people throw you a welcome back party.

You're so fat...

When you want someone to shake your hand, you have to give directions.

When you sit around the house, you sit around the house.

When I swerved to miss you, I ran out of petrol.

When you walked in front of the TV I missed three commercials.

When you were diagnosed with a flesh-eating disease, the doctor gave you 10 years to live.

You're so fat...

You're on *both* sides of the family.

When your beeper goes off, people think you're backing up.

Your driver's licence says, 'Picture continued on other side.'

The only thing you can fit into at the clothes shop is the changing room.

People jump over you rather than going around.

You're so fat...

I had to take a train and two buses just to get on your good side.

Your belly button doesn't have fluff, it has jumpers.

When you wear cord trousers, the ridges don't show.

You're half English, half Scottish and half Irish.

When you take a shower, your feet don't get wet.

You're so fat...

When you get in a lift, it has to go down.

You're so fat...

When you step on the scale it says, "One at a time please."

When you step on the scale it says, "Sorry, we don't do livestock."

You're so fat...

You were born with a silver spade in your mouth.

Chapter 4

BUMPER STICKER INSULTS

Those passive-aggressives among us like to insult people in less direct ways…via their bumper stickers.

I'd follow you anywhere, but only out of curiosity.

Some drink from the fountain of knowledge, but you just gargled.

Before you criticise someone, you should walk a mile in their shoes. That way, when you criticise them, you're a mile away and you have their shoes.

Forget about world peace.
Visualise using your indicator.

You shouldn't let your mind wander – it's too small to be let out on its own.

If stupidity hurt, you'd go through life on a morphine drip.

Keep honking...I'm reloading.

Caution! I drive like you do.

You have an inferiority complex, but not a very good one.

If what you don't know can't hurt you, you're practically invulnerable.

I'd like to help you out. Which way did you come in?

So many stupid people...so few comets.

It may be that your sole purpose in life is simply to serve as a warning to others.

I see you've got a Teflon® brain – nothing sticks.

You used to have a handle on life – but I guess it broke.

You're not a complete idiot – some parts are missing.

It IS as bad as you think and they ARE out to get you.

Good judgment comes from bad experience, and a lot of that comes from bad judgment.

Get lost in thought – it's unfamiliar territory.

There's intelligent life on this planet, but you're not it.

You've got both oars in the water, but on the same side of the boat.

Never miss a good chance to shut up.

Did the aliens forget to remove your anal probe?

You've got a party in your head, but no-one is dancing.

The switch is on, but no-one's receiving.

You're a man of few words…and you don't know what either of them mean.

If brains were taxed, you'd get a rebate.

Another dopeless hope fiend!

Where have you been all my life and why didn't you stay there?

Any similarity between you and a human is purely coincidental.

If you don't like the way I drive, stay off the footpath.

It's time to pull over and change the air in your head.

Tact is for people who aren't witty enough to be sarcastic.

Instant idiot. Just add alcohol.

I wonder if you'd drive any better if that car phone was up your butt.

There are three kinds of people: those who can count and those who can't.

The Earth is full. Go home.

They call it 'PMS' because 'mad cow disease' was already taken.

When I want your opinion, I'll beat it out of you.

You're the reason God created the middle finger.

Practise safe sex. Screw yourself.

The voices in my head don't like you.

If at first you don't succeed, you'll be a loser and a burden on society for the rest of your life.

A real gentleman wouldn't stare at my stickers.

I didn't say it was your fault. I said I'd blame you anyway.

I don't have an anger problem. I have an idiot problem.

Please take a number and stick it up your butt.

Jesus loves you. Everyone else thinks you're an arsehole.

Anyone who told you to be yourself couldn't have given you worse advice.

Please don't interrupt me while I'm ignoring you.

If I gave a shit, you'd be the first person I'd be giving it to.

You're placing a food order, not choosing life insurance.

I'm not really rude. I just say what everyone else is thinking.

What part of 'Get the hell away from me' don't you understand?

The people who don't believe in evolution are the ones that need it most.

My goal is to sleep with every man on Earth. You're the last.

Why don't you slip into something nice...like unconsciousness?

Do you still love nature, despite what it did to you?

I'm multi-tasking: listening to you and pretending I'm interested.

Rest assured. No-one gives a shit what you think.

I'm not really a proctologist but I can spot a sick arsehole when I see one.

Chapter 4

THE INSULT GRAB BAG

Sometimes, you need something a little more than just your common or garden variety insults. Do you have someone strange, pathetic, crazy, or old and wrinkly you want to have a go at? They're all here.

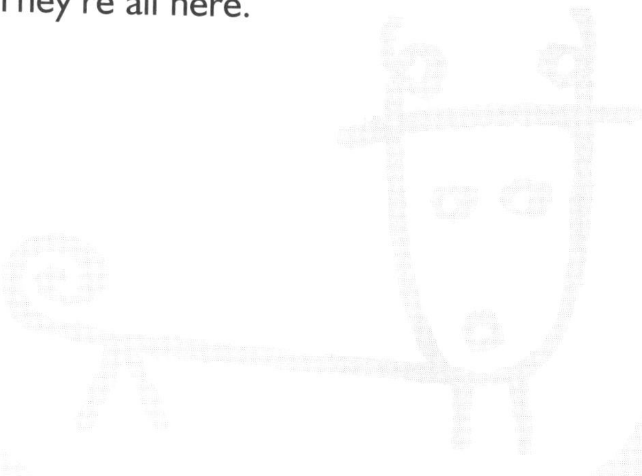

To the downright strange, you're so weird...

You get a charge out of pissing on electric fences.

To the utterly pathetic, you're so useless...

You couldn't organise a wet T-shirt competition at Playboy headquarters.

You couldn't give away presents at an orphanage at Christmas.

You couldn't sell a statue to a pigeon.

You couldn't organise a piss-up in a brewery.

You.couldn't give away condoms to a football team partying with a bunch of supermodels.

You're so useless...

You couldn't get laid if you crawled up a chicken's rear end and waited your turn.

You couldn't write dialogue for a porno movie.

You couldn't engineer your way out of a wet paper bag.

You couldn't figure it out if God gave you the instruction manual.

You're so useless...

You couldn't find two elephants if they were in the same telephone booth with you.

To the tight-fisted

To the stingy out there, watch out, or you'll be hearing these next ones…for free!

You're so cheap...

If a fly walked over your butter, you'd lick the fly.

When someone rings your doorbell, they have to yell, "Ding dong!"

On a Sunday drive you make the kids push to save petrol.

You conserve toilet paper by using both sides.

You wouldn't give away the steam off your shit.

To the old and wrinklies

To the withered-as-a-prune among us, these insults might already sound familiar…

You're so old...

An 'all-nighter' means not getting up for a piss.

Your birth certificate is in Roman numerals.

When you were at school, ancient history was called current affairs.

Your little black book contains only next-of-kin.

When you were young, the Dead Sea was just getting sick.

To the lacking in personality

Some of us have the less than perfect pleasure of being surrounded by people who have all the personality of a bowl of porridge. For those special people in our lives, here's just what to say to them:

You're as popular as a French kiss at a family reunion.

You're as welcome as a pork pie at a Jewish wedding.

You have a personality all your own... No-one else wanted it.

To the utterly psychotic

Got a slightly loopy person in your life? Forget the everyday pleasantries…cut right to the chase with these little gems.

Your ladder is missing a few rungs.

You haven't just lost the plot, you've lost the whole library.

Your cheese has slid off its cracker.

You're a teapot with a cracked lid.

You've been touched in the head, and I think it was with a jackhammer.

You're so crazy...

Your wipers don't touch the glass.

You've just bought yourself a one-way ticket on the Disoriented Express.

You're diagonally parked in a parallel universe.

You're a fruit looking for a cake to happen.

You're so crazy...

You're loopier than an onion ring.

You're closer to the edge than a bicycle on the motorway.

You got in touch with reality, but it was a bad connection.

Animal Insults

Is that your face – or are you breaking it in for a bulldog?

Romance brings out the beast in you – the jackass.

Let's play horse. I'll be the front end and you just be yourself.

Someone said that you are not fit to sleep with pigs. I stuck up for the pigs.

The last time I saw a face like yours I threw it a fish.

The wheel is turning but the hamster is definitely dead.

I heard...

That they tried to take an X-ray picture of your jaw, but all they got was a moving picture.

That you were a lady-killer – they take one look at you and die of shock.

That when you were born, your father threw rocks at the stork.

That you went to the haunted house and they offered you a job.

That you got a brain transplant and the brain rejected you.

That you went to have your head examined, but the doctors found nothing there.

That you went to see the doctor and told him that you wanted a little wart removed; so he had you thrown out of his office.

We know...

That you would go to the end of the world for us. But would you stay there?

That you would give your life for us. Promise!

That you could not live without us. We'll pay for the funeral.

That I understand you. I just seem to have a way with dumb animals.

That whatever kind of look you were going for, you missed.

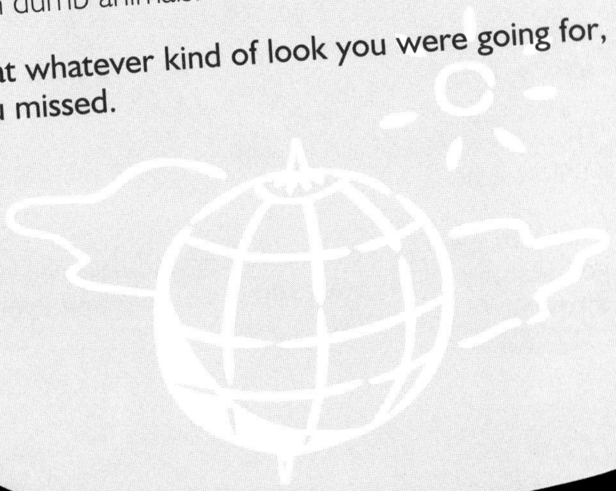

Ugly, Dumb, Rude and Annoying

We think of you when we are lonely. Then we are content to be alone.

Was it hard learning to be so ugly or were you a quick learner?

I'm trying to see things from your perspective, but I can't seem to get my head up my butt as far as you can.

We all spring from apes, but you didn't spring far enough.

I may be fat, but you're ugly, and I can diet.

You're not acting like yourself lately. I noticed the improvement immediately.

Insult Quotes

"The way to procure insults is to submit to them: a man meets with no more respect than he exacts."
William Hazlitt

"I feel so miserable without you. It's almost like having you here."
Stephen Bishop

"He is a self-made man and worships his creator."
John Bright

"He has all the virtues I dislike and none of the vices I admire."
Winston Churchill

Insult Quotes

"The first human who hurled an insult instead of a stone was the founder of civilisation."
Sigmund Freud

"A modest little person, with much to be modest about."
Winston Churchill

"I've just learned about his illness. Let's hope it's nothing trivial."
Irvin S. Cobb

"A husband should not insult his wife publicly, at parties. He should insult her in the privacy of the home."
James Thurber

Insult Quotes

"No-one can make you feel inferior without your consent."
Eleanor Roosevelt

"It belongs to human nature to hate those you have injured."
Agricola Tacitus

"It is often better not to see an insult than to avenge it."
Seneca

"They don't hardly make 'em like him any more – but just to be on the safe side, he should be castrated anyway."
Hunter S. Thompson

"I've had a perfectly wonderful evening. But this wasn't it."
Groucho Marx

Insult Quotes

"One may be continually abusive without saying anything just; but one cannot be always laughing at a man, without now and then stumbling on something witty."
Jane Austen

"If a man's character is to be abused, say what you will, there's nobody like a relation to do the business."
William Makepeace Thackeray

"Reader, suppose you were an idiot; and suppose you were a member of Congress; but I repeat myself."
Mark Twain

"I was married by a judge. I should have asked for a jury."
Groucho Marx

Self-abuse

"I don't know anything about music. In my line you don't have to."
Elvis Presley

"I go from stool to stool in singles bars hoping to get lucky, but there's never any gum under any of them."
Emo Phillips

"A 'Bay Area Bisexual' told me I didn't quite coincide with either of her desires."
Woody Allen

"For birth control I rely on my personality."
Milt Abel

Shakespearean Insults

"Where will thou find a cavern dark enough to mask thy monstrous visage."
Julius Caesar

"Sense sure you have, else could you not have motion; but sure that sense is apoplex'd."
Hamlet

"What cracker is this same that deafs our ears with this abundance of superfluous breath."
King John

"If thou dost marry, I'll give thee this plague for thy dowry."
Hamlet

"[Thy] kiss is comfortless as frozen water to a starved snake."
Troilus and Cressida

More Shakespearean Insults

"Hence, horrible villain, or I'll spurn thine eyes like balls before me; I'll unhair thy head, Thou shalt be whipp'd with wire, and stew'd in brine, smarting in lingering pickle."
Antony and Cleopatra

"God hath given you one face and you make yourselves another."
Hamlet

"As I told you always, her beauty and her brain go not together."
Cymbeline

"In civility thou seem'st so empty."
As You Like It

Yet More Shakespearean Insults

"Thou art essentially a natural coward without instinct."
Henry IV, part I

"You have such a February face, so full of frost, of storm and cloudiness."
Much Ado About Nothing

"[Thou art] a most notable coward, an infinite and endless liar, an hourly promise breaker, the owner of no one good quality."
All's Well That Ends Well

"Hang cur, hang, you whoreson, insolent noisemaker."
The Tempest

"Degenerate and base art thou."
The Two Gentlemen of Verona

Concoct your own Shakespearean insult.

Choose a word from each column and preface each insult with 'Thou':

bawdy	bat-fowling	baggage
beslubbering	beef-witted	barnacle
churlish	boil-brained	boar-pig
clouted	clay-brained	bum-bailey
craven	common-kissing	canker-blossom
droning	doghearted	codpiece
errant	dread-bolted	death-token
fawning	earth-vexing	dewberry
fobbing	elf-skinned	flap-dragon
frothy	fen-sucked	flirt-gill
infectious	full-gorged	haggard

loggerheaded	half-faced	hedge-pig
lumpish	hasty-witted	horn-beast
paunchy	ill-breeding	lout
puking	knotty-pated	malt-worm
puny	milk-livered	mammet
rank	onion-eyed	minnow
roguish	pottle-deep	moldwarp
saucy	reeling-ripe	nut-hook
spongy	rude-growing	pignut
warped	tickle-brained	varlot
wayward	toad-spotted	vassal
yeasty	weather-bitten	wagtail

Brains

But you did get a brain that day. The problem is that you should have asked for one to take away.

You got your brain very early. Apparently the warranty has run out.

Brains aren't everything. In fact, in your case they're nothing.

When they were handing out brains you arrived too late, all you got was a rain check.

Don't think, it might sprain your brain.

They had ran out of brains by the time you got there, so they gave you a nice wood carving instead.

You have one brain cell and it's fighting for dominance.

Great Retorts

Lady Astor, to Winston Churchill: "If I were married to you, I'd put poison in your coffee."
Winston Churchill: "If you were my wife, I'd drink it."

Lord Sandwich: "Really, Mr. Wilkes, I don't know whether you'll die on the gallows or of the pox."
John Wilkes: "That depends, my lord, on whether I embrace your principles or your mistress."

Wife of prominent politician to Winston Churchill (with distain in her voice): "Mr. Churchill, you are drunk!"
Mr. Churchill: "Yes, madam, and you are ugly. But in the morning, I will be sober, and you will still be ugly."

Noel Coward to Edna Ferber, who was wearing a tailored suit: "You look almost like a man."
Edna Ferber: "So do you."

Oscar Wilde

"A man who moralises is usually a hypocrite, and a woman who moralises is invariably plain."

"She is a peacock in everything but beauty."

"Some cause happiness wherever they go; others whenever they go."

"He has no enemies, but is intensely disliked by his friends."

"There is so much to be said in favour of modern journalism. By giving us the opinions of the uneducated it keeps us in touch with the ignorance of the community."

Oscar Wilde

"I like Wagner's music better than anybody's. It is so loud that one can talk the whole time without other people hearing what one says."

"I like hearing myself talk. It is one of my greatest pleasures. I often have long conversations with myself, and I am so clever that sometimes I don't understand a single word of what I am saying."

"If you haven't got anything nice to say about anybody, then come and sit next to me."

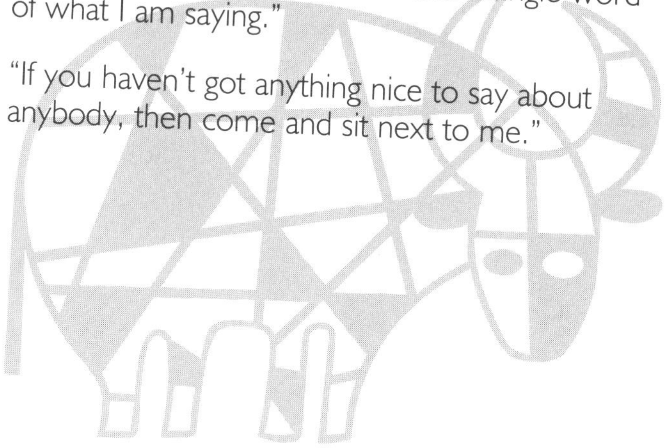

Put Downs

“He is racist, he’s homophobic, he’s xenophobic and he’s a sexist. He’s the perfect Republican candidate.”
Bill Press (about Pat Buchanan)

“Most of the time he sounds like he has a mouth full of wet toilet paper.”
Rex Reed (about Marlon Brando)

“An agile but unintelligent and abnormal German, possessed of the mania of grandeur.”
Leo Tolstoy (about Friedrich Nietzsche)

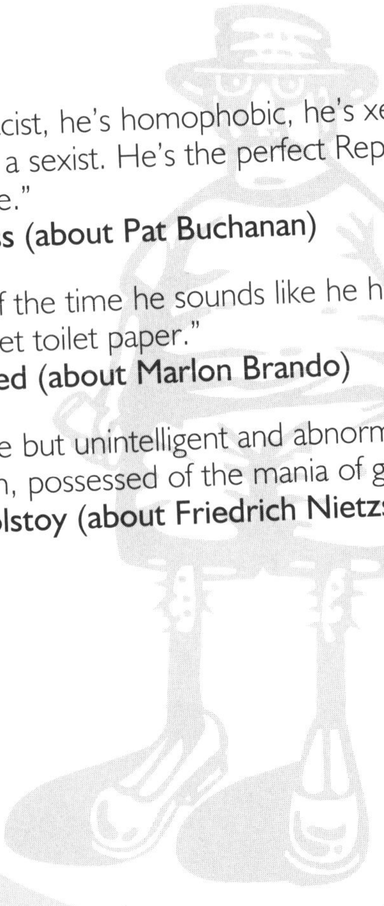

"The plain truth is, that he was a most intolerable ruffian, a disgrace to human nature, and a blot of blood and grease upon the history of England."
Charles Dickens (about Henry VIII)

"Nothing but old fags and cabbage-stumps of quotations from the Bible and the rest, stewed in the juice of deliberate, journalistic dirty-mindedness."
DH Lawrence (about James Joyce)

Quick and Nasty

I was just about to do my moron impression, but you beat me to it.

Do you have a bad back? Because your front's not all that good either.

Hey, I might not be the cutest guy here, but I am the only one talking to you.

I'm trying to imagine you with a personality.

Why don't you slip into something more comfortable...like a coma.

I never forget a face – but in your case I'll make an exception.